SKYROCKET YOUR SUCCESS

10 KEYS TO REFOCUS, REPOSITION & RECLAIM YOUR PURPOSE

QUEASHAR L. HALLIBURTON

Copyright © 2019 by Queashar L. Halliburton

Editor- Tenita C. Johnson

All rights reserved. No part of this publication may be reproduced, distributed, or transmitted in any form or by any means, including photocopying, recording, or other electronic or mechanical methods, without the prior written permission of the publisher, except in the case of brief quotations embodied in critical reviews and certain other noncommercial uses permitted by copyright law. For permission requests, write to the publisher, addressed "Attention: Permissions Coordinator," at the address below.

ISBN   9781733549509   (Paperback)
ISBN   978-1-7335495-1-6   (eBook)
Library of Congress Control Number: 2019931700

Queashar Detroit Publishing, LLC
P.O. Box 201126
Ferndale, MI 48220
www.sharhalliburton.com

Ordering Information:
Quantity sales. Special discounts are available on quantity purchases by corporations, associations, and others. For details, contact the publisher at the address above.
Orders by U.S. trade bookstores and wholesalers.

Printed in the United States of America

TABLE OF CONTENTS

Acknowledgments 5

Dedication 7

Introduction 10

Chapter 1 The Definition of Success 16

Chapter 2 Affirmations for Success 28

Chapter 3 The Keys to Success 34

Chapter 4 The Habits of Successful People: Roll Call 46

Chapter 5 The Habits of the Unsuccessful 54

Chapter 6 The Truth About Success 60

Chapter 7 Deficiencies 68

Chapter 8 Self Sabotaging Behaviors that Delay Success ... 80

Chapter 9 A Modern Day Study on Success 94

Chapter 10 Maintaining Success 110

Chapter 11 Ten Keys to Refocus, Reposition & Reclaim Your Purpose! 112

ACKNOWLEDGMENTS

First, I would like to thank my Lord and Savior, Jesus Christ, for life, health and strength. I have such a supportive family. My mother, Jarita R. Barge-Halliburton has always been such a great inspiration for writing. I got my love of writing from her. She is truly my rock. My siblings, Shergora, Lisa, Cornelius Jr. and Kellie have always encouraged me, as well. Many thanks to my accountability partner and great friend, Mona Reed, for all your support throughout the years.

I'd like to also give a special thanks to three people who I have met through social media. It's amazing that I have received so much support and gained so much knowledge from you. My tribe is lit! Shout out to Tenita C. Johnson, my editor; Dr. De'Andrea Matthews, my mentor; and Stephanie Rodnez of Godlywood Girl for your Writer's Academy and for all your support. I'd like to thank all those who took out time to help me with research for this book by completing a survey. I appreciate you. This has been an amazing journey and I can't wait to see what the future holds!

DEDICATION

This book is dedicated to the memory of my late father, Cornelius Earl Halliburton, Sr. He was such a hard worker who had so many unfulfilled dreams. I get some of my entrepreneurial ideas from him. He worked at Chrysler and he also loved to cook. He always wanted to own a diner. His life was cut short at the young age of 43. He never got to see the success he dreamed about. It is my goal to continue to make him proud. Rest peacefully, Dad. I love you!

    I also want to dedicate this book to women who feel trapped by life's circumstances, whether it be because of past mistakes, family responsibilities, or just a lack of motivation. My goal is to inspire and motivate you to use your God-given gifts and talents and make your dream a reality. Don't put your gifts on the back burner. It's never too late to reach your full potential. If there is breath in your lungs, there is still time to fulfill your life's dreams and desires.

With love,
Queashar L. Halliburton

Queashar L. Halliburton

INTRODUCTION

"I just can't do this anymore! It's just too frustrating," I said to my boss.

"Well, Queashar, you just have to keep trying until you pass. You're intelligent. You have a degree. You can do this. Just focus and keep studying. You'll pass the next time," my boss said.

"Well, this is just too much. I'm not going through this anymore. It's just too stressful," I said.

I'd taken the Insurance Property & Casualty test a couple of times before and missed passing by only a couple questions. My boss was so encouraging, though. He was an award-winning insurance agent with decades of experience. He knew the insurance industry well and thought that I would be a great asset to his agency.

"Maybe you just need to go home and relax. Just go home and relax today and, tomorrow, start studying again. Take your test results print out and focus on the area that you did not pass," he told me. Then, I decided to let my boss off the hook.

"I passed!" I said, laughing hysterically.

"Queashar, I knew you could do it!" he said with the biggest smile on his face.

His eyes got big and he let out a hearty full laugh. He was elated, but not more than me. I had found a new career. I was so eager to dive in and "take the bull by the horns" with this new career. I finally felt that I was in a career where I could help people and make a difference. From the moment I stepped into the insurance office, I saw Agent of the Month and Agent of the Year plaques scattered across the walls.

I knew that, one day, my picture and name would be included on the infamous Wall of Fame. I was going to make a positive contribution. I was going to be the number one go-to insurance girl for all the local dealerships. Since I was a former salesperson, I knew it would be easy to gain business from the sales people at my former dealership. I just needed to get to the other dealerships and make my name and services known.

I loved this new opportunity! I was going to learn whatever I could to advance in my new career. I was going to be like a sponge, soaking up every opportunity that was afforded to me. I was going to make this work for me.

I was a bright-eyed, 27-year-old who was full of enthusiasm and energy, and I had finally found my niche.

"Success is just around the corner," I said to myself.

Take a leap of faith and soar!

Forget all about your failures!

It's a great day to start over!

Reclaim your purpose!

CHAPTER 1

The Definition of Success

How do you define success? Is it defined by how much money you make? Is success determined by how many people you influence or how many followers you have on social media? Is it defined by how many awards or public accolades you receive?

Many people define success differently. Some believe success is defined by the attainment of a substantial monetary amount. Some believe that success is realized once you accomplish a lifelong goal. I believe that success is continuous achievement or goal attainment. The achievement of success is an ongoing cycle. It never stops, even when we meet our lifelong goals.

When we think in terms of success, we tend to focus on big accomplishments and yet, forget about our small victories along the way. For instance, if we are working on a major project for work, sometimes we seem overwhelmed with the completion of the project in its entirety. However, when we break the task down into smaller steps, the bigger picture seems more attainable.

Success is not measured by the size of the goal. It does not have to be a big goal for it to be considered success. Any progress in the positive direction of your target goal will eventually breed success.

I've always had a deep admiration for high achievers. I love the cycle of achievement. Some people are just happy to have a job. However, simply working a job was never enough for me. I wanted to experience career fulfillment. I wanted to feel like I was making a difference in this world.

After graduating with a Bachelor of Arts in Communications from Michigan State University, I had a big dream of becoming a public relations professional. I'd completed public relations internships, and I'd even envisioned my new life as a public relations executive. I found a job as a public relations assistant at a local firm and thought I was on my way to a successful career in PR.

Well, as soon as I got comfortable, I was laid off. I had worked six months on the job, and I was devastated. I applied to many marketing and PR firms. Yet, due to my lack of corporate experience, I never landed my dream PR job. I knew I had to pay bills, so I was on the hunt for a new career.

A friend told me that Southfield Public Schools was looking for substitute teachers. I applied for the job and was hired in September of 1997. I loved this new job! God blessed me to have an assignment every day for two years. I mostly had long-term projects. I met some great people and loved teaching.

I even attempted to go back to school and get my teacher's certification. I got accepted to both University of Detroit and Marygrove College, but I decided not to pursue the secondary education degree at the time because I didn't want to incur any more debt with student loans. I decided to find a new career that would provide a decent living instead. I would revisit furthering my education later.

Since I was not a permanent teacher, I didn't get paid in the summer months. In the summer of 1998, I qualified for unemployment. But, the summer of 1999 was a different story. I did not qualify because of the promise to return to teaching in the fall of 1999.

Another career was calling my name. I had just purchased my first car from Mel Farr Ford in Oak Park, Michigan. My sales associate told me that he thought I would be a good fit for car sales. I agreed and, since I was off for the summer, I needed to make some money. I was a good influencer and I always had the gift of gab. I was up for a new challenge.

I filled out an application. I scheduled an interview and I was excited. I wanted to work at the Oak Park location because it was lively. It seemed like the place to be. I received a call from the new car sales manager at the Ferndale location. I went to the interview and was hired on the spot. I loved my job. I learned some great closing skills and made some lifelong friends.

A few months into my job at Mel Farr, I met an insurance agent named Aretha Johnson. She worked as an agent at an insurance agency in Southfield. Aretha was the go-to agent for auto insurance needs for my clients. She was friendly, efficient and professional. She seemed to love her job and she saw something in me that would be a great fit for the insurance field.

One day, she pulled me to the side and asked me if I would be interested in becoming an insurance agent. She said that she had already talked to her boss about me, and he wanted me to come to his office to meet him.

I gave it some serious thought. Then, I thought to myself, If I could sell new and used cars at Mel Farr, then surely, insurance would be an easier sell.

One day at lunchtime, I went to meet Aretha's boss. I picked a great day to visit his office. His office was booming and lively. The agency owner gave me an interview on the spot and told me that I could start the following Monday. I gave my job immediate notice and began my new career in insurance sales. It was a good time for me to exit the dealership because there were many structural changes going on at the time. It was a smooth transition to my new career.

Learning the new business of insurance was quite challenging. Getting licensed was tough. But, after studying and receiving great mentorship from the agency, I passed my test and gained my property and casualty licensing in September of 2000. I had found a new career and was happy with my choice. I didn't search for this career. It found me.

I worked at the agency for many years and learned a lot about the field of insurance. I learned about being persistent and never taking the first, "No" for an answer, without asking for a second opportunity to close the sale. Working at this agency was my first real experience with success. I was really making a difference and helping to educate consumers about the importance of asset protection.

Throughout my insurance sales career, I won multiple awards. I've earned Agent of the Month several times, and even Agent of the Year a few times. I've won multiple agency contests, which included great prizes like suite tickets to the Tigers and Pistons games. I've even won a few trips to places like Disney World and Vancouver, British Columbia.

You may start out with one career preference and end up doing something that you've never imagined. You must be willing to learn and adapt to many different work environments. Accept plan B if your plan A doesn't materialize.

Although, I never experienced success in the career of my choice, I've had some worthwhile internships, and volunteer opportunities with political candidates, musical artists and authors that gave me rewarding experiences in public relations.

You must be patient and know that your journey to success will not always be easy. I've had some interesting twists and turns that made me question if I would ever be able to achieve the level of success that I desired in life.

A good education is not an automatic golden ticket to success. You must work hard and be strategic to achieve success. Nothing will be given to you. Sometimes, you must take a job that you don't want just to pay bills and sustain your family. Eventually, you will find your niche and become the success story you've always dreamed of.

To date, I have been a licensed agent for more than 18 years. I am currently employed at a non-profit health insurance company in the Detroit metropolitan area. Although this was not my career of choice, I took the opportunity that was presented to me. I dug my heels in and learned the business, and I have achieved success as an insurance agent.

Throughout my career, I've worked in many industries, including education, insurance, construction management, real estate and public relations. Success in the business world is quite challenging at times. If you stay focused, with prayer, networking and hard work, you can achieve success in any field.

Everybody has growing pains, but most people only highlight the good times. Don't feel bad if you think your journey to success isn't immediate! It takes time, hard work and dedication to make it to the top. Be patient and continue to work hard, and your time will come. In this book, I will discuss how identifying your unique purpose will help you focus on your success and deter you from comparing, and secretly competing with others.

This book was written to encourage professional women who have courted success, but have not reached their fullest potential in the field of their choice. You may have done all the right things that you were told to do to become successful, like pursuing a quality education and working hard in corporate America. You may have even taken a few risks to take your career to the next level. But something is still missing. You may have experienced a certain level of success. But, in your heart, there is so much more to accomplish.

You may have experienced sleepless nights because you are not operating in your God-given gifts. You have hopes and dreams of making a great impact in life. You may be nowhere near pursuing your dream career or achieving your personal goals. You may have cried yourself to sleep night after night because you are unfulfilled.

You may feel like you've done your part, but you feel out of place in corporate America because you were called and purposed to be an entrepreneur. If this is you, I understand and feel your pain. I have been there and done that for decades. I know how you feel. You have worked hard, but you still haven't seen your dreams fulfilled. It appears that everyone else is achieving greatness; yet, you just feel mediocre. It's your time to shine. I hope this book encourages you to step out on faith and stop letting negative self-talk, and other self-sabotaging behaviors, stop you from the personal success that you've hoped, dreamed and prayed for.

Here's to your success!

Queashar L. Halliburton

CHAPTER 2

Affirmations for Success

As a born-again believer, I believe any success that I achieve in life is because I have a solid foundation in my relationship with God. A solid foundation and prayer life are the reasons why I am here. So, when I have a desire to accomplish an important goal, the first thing I do is pray about it. I pray that God will give me clarity and wisdom regarding how to accomplish the goal. After I pray, I begin to write out a plan. The Bible tells us to write the vision and make it plain (Habakkuk 2:2). You must have a vision to accomplish success.

To be excellent in your gift, you must be anointed and appointed to perform your purpose or gift. What has God purposed you to do in this life? You must discover your purpose in life. God has blessed each one of us with purpose. Is there something that you feel you are called to do, but you are afraid to pursue? Is there something you dream about doing in your career, but you keep putting that desire to the wayside?

That thing that you dream about, or that thing that you constantly have the urge to do, is your calling in life. Stop being afraid to pursue it. Go after your dreams. Forget about what family or friends will say. Just pursue it after praying about it. If it is meant to be, with your hard work, it will come to fruition.

AFFIRMATIONS FOR SUCCESS

Everything I touch will prosper.

I must be successful. There is no other option.

I am prepared to succeed in anything I want to accomplish.

I will make my dreams my reality. All my hard work will pay off.

I am who God says I am. I am fearfully and intrinsically made in His image. I am a success story, waiting to be revealed.

I am a success story!

Success will follow me all the days of my life.

I am a success story, waiting to unfold.

My past doesn't define me.

I am a success story, waiting to unfold.

My past failures helped to build my character.

I am a success story, waiting to unfold.

I am the picture of success.

I am a success story, waiting to unfold.

I refuse to think negatively.

I am a success story, waiting to unfold.

When I glance in the mirror in the morning,

I am a success story, waiting to unfold.

When I get dressed for work,

I am a success story, waiting to unfold.

When I receive a late student loan notice,

I am a success story, waiting to unfold.

When my bank account is not where it needs it to be,

I am a success story, waiting to unfold.

When I get a negative report from my doctor,

I am a success story, waiting to unfold.

Success will follow me all the days of my life.

I am Queashar Lanay Halliburton,

and

I am a success story, waiting to unfold.

*Recite this aloud, but replace my name with yours.

No matter what we go through in life, we must maintain positivity and proclaim success. No matter the situation, claim that it will work out for your good. Be positive and maintain a positive mindset, even in the face of adversity, and success will follow.

-Queashar Lanay Halliburton

Queashar L. Halliburton

CHAPTER 3

The Keys to Success

What does it take to become successful? Hard work. Dedication. Consistently and constantly educating yourself in your field will keep you at the top of your game. You must be disciplined and consistent. You must be in the right frame of mind to be successful.

Being successful is not an easy feat. You must be bold, brave and confident in every task you complete. You must have tenacity and never give up on your dreams. You must be authentic and know who you are. Most importantly, you must keep learning your craft and stay relevant in your field. Let's look at these concepts a little more closely. First, we'll look at discipline and consistency.

Discipline & Consistency

The ability to be strategic in creating a routine and sticking to the routine until the plan is complete is what will make you successful. You must be consistent in your tasks, to complete them. You must select a time that works within your schedule. You have to literally schedule things and put it on your calendar. Even when you don't feel like it, you must work toward completing that goal. Something will always come up. You must fight through feelings of laziness and get out of your comfort zone. Create a routine and be strategic about following the steps consistently. Success will follow. Consistency is a great challenge for me, at times. I never have a problem with creativity, but consistency is an issue for me. I would often start a project, then get bored with the routine and mundane tasks. I had to learn to do it anyway so that I could celebrate the completion of a task. I tend to be impatient. I want things to be done quickly. I had to learn to be patient and go through the process.

Mindset Matters

A positive mindset sets you up for success. A negative mindset sets you up for failure. Whatever you do in life, it first starts as a thought in your mind. You must be able to dream it to achieve it. You must allow your mind to believe that you can achieve a goal. You are the pilot of your positive thinking. You must have the willpower to think positively and make your dream a reality. Once you set your mind to accomplish something, negative thoughts will surface. You must be able to fight off negative thoughts. When you are faced with a negative thought, don't entertain it. If you do entertain the negative thought, it will plant a seed of negativity and start growing.

Negative thoughts always tried to invade my mind. At first, I tried to stay positive and not dwell on the negative thoughts. For instance, I would get a great idea and start gathering information. After gathering the info, I made plans to make the great idea a reality. Then, I would hit roadblocks or situations that would make the idea more complicated.

Then, I would lose interest. I started thinking of anything that could and would go wrong. I had so many questions. I felt like the problem was insurmountable. I got caught up in the details and it became too much of a burden. I embraced the negative thoughts and put the plan on hold.

Be Bold, Brave & Confident

You already have what you need to be successful in life. To be successful, you must be bold and brave. You must be willing to do the things that the average person isn't willing to do. It takes guts to make it big in this world. Don't be afraid to be different. There are so many counterfeits running around, acting like they are legitimate. You must be confident and secure enough to believe that you will be successful, no matter what it takes. Being bold, brave and confident is essential when you are following your dream. You must be strong enough to still go after your dream, even when Negative Nancy tells you that what you want to do is not the way to go. Be confident in your calling and pursue it aggressively. Learn your specialty and know it like the back of your hand. Keep learning until you are recognized as an authority in your field.

Embrace & Celebrate Change

Let's face it. To grow, we must embrace and celebrate change. If we do things the same way, we will never get ahead in life. We would simply go around in circles, without forward advancement. Change is what produces growth. We must create new ways to accomplish our goals. Be innovative. If you are in business, you must be flexible. Business trends are constantly growing and changing.

Never Give Up

It will get hard, but don't fold. There will be times when you just want to give up. The difference between a successful person and an unsuccessful person is the will not to give up. A successful person knows when to take a break, but they won't totally give in to failure. They will find a new way to accomplish a goal once they experience resistance in the process.

During my journey as a new entrepreneur, there have been multiple times where I just felt lost. I have felt like giving up because I was so frustrated with the learning curve when it came to certain aspects of business. I sometimes felt like I should do a disappearing act and just shrink back into a cave. I felt like I should just forget all about having my own business. But then, I thought about why I wanted to pursue my dream. Then, I got clarity again. That is what keeps me going. I can call my own shots. It's so empowering to know I can have the dream job that I've always wanted because I am free to create what I desire. It's so empowering when you decide to create your own dream. You must tap into your heart's desire and make your dream your reality. When you realize your power to create the life you want, and do the things to make it happen, it makes life so much more fulfilling and enjoyable. Be brave and honest with what you want in this life. Explore, research, design and create the life and business you want.

Be Authentic

Don't be a copycat. Be you! Stop trying to be like the next person. When you imitate another person, you are not being genuine. What works for someone else will not always work for you. When you are trying to be like the next person, you are being a thief. You are robbing yourself of the true blessing that is realized when you are the true person that you were made to be. What makes you think that you are not good enough? When God created you, He created a masterpiece. Why are you afraid to show the real you, the quirky you? Embrace your differences. No two people are alike, not even identical twins. Their DNA is different. You must be who God made and called you to be. You are valuable. No one has the same experience that you have. No one has your understanding or point of view. We must not be afraid to embrace our authentic selves. Show the world what you're working with. We all have innovative mindsets and unique viewpoints. Be you and shine. Your uniqueness is what will stand out and attract your tribe. Look in the mirror and point out all the things that make you different. Call them out and say to yourself, "I am beautiful. God made me this way for a reason. I will embrace my authentic differences, and I will share my experience through my voice. I will not duplicate the next person."

You must love yourself unconditionally. Perfect being you. God made you as a unique work of art for a purpose. Love the way you look and rock with it, no matter what. Embrace all of you. You are a combination of your parents' DNA. □

Keep Learning

Keep learning and become an expert in your specialty. One thing that you can always count on is that the world is infinite. There is always something new for you to learn. Keep learning, even after you meet all of your goals. Make new goals and follow the same steps that helped you achieve success. You already know they work. Commit to learning something new every week. There are a million things created every day. What is something that you want to learn? Each week set aside time to explore something new in your industry. Take risks and try something new. It will give you a new perspective and it will allow you to grow mentally. Once you learn something new, you will be able to share your experience with someone else. It will be exciting to share your new findings with a great friend.

Queashar L. Halliburton

Invest in yourself today.

Three to five years from now you

will be glad that you did.

Queashar L. Halliburton

CHAPTER 4

The Habits of Successful People: Roll Call

Successful people awaken early. They get their day started before the average person gets out of bed. Jack Dorsey, co-founder of Twitter and Square, wakes up at 5 a.m. He starts his day with meditation and exercises, like jogging. Investor and philanthropist, Warren Buffet, wakes up at 6:45 a.m. He knows the importance of reading and, according to Business Insider Magazine, he makes sure that he reads at least 500 pages daily.

Media mogul, Oprah Winfrey, wakes up before dawn to meditate. According to Business Insider Magazine, when former first lady, Michelle Obama, was in the White House, she started her day with a morning work out before 5 a.m. Most successful people are focused and strategic when it comes to managing their time. They have an established daily routine.

Successful people also have some distinguishing habits. They are methodic and intentional about all things. They understand that nothing just happens. They are obsessed with tackling their day. They plan their success ahead of time. They create and follow a pattern of learned behavior that continues to reap success. Most successful people have a morning routine. They get up early. They pray, meditate or concentrate on the intentions for the next day. Successful people handle the complicated tasks first, and then delegate the tasks that are not their specialty.

Successful people take time to read in the morning, whether it be the Bible or books about business or motivation. Some listen to motivational podcasts or sermons, and recite or listen to positive affirmations before they start their day. These habits keep them pumped and motivated. These affirmations feed them spiritually.

The thing that keeps them going is consistency and discipline. They have mastered the art of doing the same routine repeatedly because their established patterns bring them continual success. Successful people are willing to do the things that the average person refuses to do. Successful people have the mindset of victory. They know that success is the reward of consistent action.

Successful people have a focused mindset and a positive outlook on life. They have tunnel vision. They have already envisioned their success from the start of a task. When successful people are in the planning stages, they plan with the desired end in mind. They have already rid themselves of the obstacles mentally. They have trained their minds to automatically think positively, even in difficult times and tasks. They know from history that if they are consistent in their routine, success will follow. They don't waste time overthinking the situation. They make quick, confident moves. They rarely second guess themselves. They strategically analyze the situation and move forward. This is one of the skills that makes them so successful. They simplify the process.

Successful people help others achieve greatness. They usually are not stingy with knowledge. They understand that once they become successful, they must reach back and help someone else achieve greatness through the power of mentorship. They are not overprotective or secretive about sharing their ideas or strategies.

Successful people love learning new things. They embrace education and find innovative ways to accomplish their goals. They look at learning as a stepping stone, not an obstacle. They understand that learning is the key to growth and prosperity.

Successful people understand that, sometimes, there is wisdom in silence. They know that, through active listening, they can learn a lot. They are willing to let others thoroughly express a complete thought, without interrupting them.

Successful people aren't intimidated by sharing the limelight with others. They find it rewarding to give others credit for triumphs and wins. They are secure and they know that some things are better accomplished and celebrated when they work as a team.

Successful people learn from their mistakes. They aren't afraid to make mistakes because they understand that failure will eventually lead to success. Failure helps them acknowledge what doesn't work; therefore, it makes them more resourceful. Failure allows them to find new ways and new methods to solve problems.

Successful people are adaptable to change. They understand that change is inevitable. They understand that change promotes growth and adds another dimension of possibilities. They look at the holistic approach and understand that the world is ever changing. Successful people have ambition that propels them to the next level. They know that it takes dedication and willpower to succeed. Most successful people have a disdain for mediocrity. They are not satisfied with the status quo. They feel a sense of entitlement that pulls them into the winners circle. They want to gain the prize of success. Work ethic and dedication make all the difference between a successful person and the unsuccessful person.

Success is more than just

a seven-letter word.

It's a journey of self-discovery.

CHAPTER 5

The Habits of the Unsuccessful

On the other side of the coin lies unsuccessful people. Unsuccessful people are always complaining about life's circumstances, but they are not willing to work to change those circumstances. They are easily irritated and they, more times than not, settle for the easy route. They are always looking for shortcuts. They are happy with the status quo. They make decisions based on their current situation. They are not as risky as a successful person. They are predictable and make safe decisions. They may be easily unmotivated, and they are okay if things remain the same. They fear change and growth.

The unsuccessful person is always pointing the finger. The blame game is king. It's never their fault when things unfold negatively. It's always the next person's fault. Their chronic pessimistic attitude is the reason why people walk in the opposite direction when they enter a room. They feel entitled to all the great things in life, but aren't willing to put in the long hours to finish the project.

Unsuccessful people don't know how to prioritize their day. They just play it by ear. Whichever way the wind blows helps them determine the agenda for the day. They are inspired by their mood, and that very mood determines how their day will be. If they wake up on the wrong side of the bed with a negative attitude, that will set the tone for their day. Unsuccessful people are not proactive when it comes to handling business. They always put things off. They do what they are forced to do. No plans are needed. Whatever happens, happens.

Unsuccessful people hang around people without vision. They don't think about how their actions will affect the future. They are reactive instead of proactive. They thrive on negative energy. Their next move is determined by the actions of others. They are not intuitive; they are followers, not leaders. What they do in life is determined by what other people do in theirs. They don't think for themselves. They are always worried about what someone else thinks and how they look in the eyes of others.

Unsuccessful people constantly multitask and let others control their time. They are always doing too much so that it seems as if they are busy. They are busy going in multiple directions, with no real destination in sight. They move in a circular motion and they are full of confusion. They lack focus, but they are sure to always let people know that they are on the move.

They embrace procrastination as their safety net. It guarantees that things are always the same. They love being comfortable. Unsuccessful people specialize in wasting time. They always encourage others to take their time to complete a task because, after all, you deserve to relax. The unsuccessful person always conforms to the status quo. After all, there is no reason to reinvent the wheel. The process is already set and that's just the way it is. There is no need to change things up. It worked for the others, so why should they waste their time tweaking something that is already working?

The unsuccessful person is judgmental and loves to hold grudges. They are attracted to drama and they always look to pull people into their emotional roller coaster. They don't map out their day. Any thought will control their day and they will be moving in all kinds of directions.

Success doesn't require you to be perfect. It only requires that you are consistently committed to taking steps toward accomplishing your goals.

Queashar L. Halliburton

CHAPTER 6

The Truth about Success: The Good and the Bad

When you think of success, do you only think about the positive side of success? Most people automatically think about the money, cars, fame, circle of upwardly mobile friends, jet-setting and the like. Success has both a good and bad side to it. While on the journey to success, you can miss a lot personally and socially.

One of the down sides to success includes long, lonely nights working late, while everyone else seems to be having a great time socially.

However, success is not free. It takes early mornings, long nights and hard work to become a success. Friends may not understand why you are working so hard. They may try to tell you to just relax and finish that project tomorrow. Friends and family may tell you that they think you are doing too much because they don't understand your end game.

Here are a few ways that your life can change when you start pursuing success.

1.   *The road to success can sometimes seem lonely*. If you want to be successful, you must be willing to step out of the limelight for a while. You will not be able to be on the scene like you used to be. You will need to take time to hone your craft and master your trade. You want to stand out and make a difference in your industry. You will miss many celebrations. You will miss hanging out with family and friends. If you are always working, your circle may leave you behind if they don't understand where your focus lies. Many successful business people have small circles of friends who may be able to understand the process, but you may lose some, too.

You will work late nights and early mornings. When you are pursuing success, sometimes, you may be the last one to leave the office. There have been times in my career that I was the last one to leave. I was still working and everyone else was out the door at 5 p.m. I always stayed behind because I wanted to finish my to-do list for the day and prepare for the next day. As an insurance agent, many times, prospects were only interested if you got right back to them. I couldn't afford to wait until the next day to reach out. Waiting could cause me to lose the sale. I had to be willing to put in the extra time to close the deal. This practice was successful for me and allowed me to constantly win the "Agent of the Month" award back to back at the agency.

2. **The pursuit of success can cause anxiety and stress**. It can cause you to feel overwhelmed at times. The pursuit of success causes immediate worry. In my study, 50 percent of people revealed that they sometimes feel anxious about their success. Some anxiety regarding success is normal. It keeps you on your toes and striving to be great. I think that a normal amount of anxiety helps to keep us grounded.

3. **You may not take care of yourself as much because you may become obsessed with success**. Your health may suffer in your pursuit of success. You may miss

your yearly doctors' visits if you are overconsumed with work or projects. You may ignore small aches and pains along the way, as well.

4. **The desire to be successful may cause one to take risks on investments.** In the business world, those that are successful are willing to take risks. If they feel that there is a possibility for growth, they may indulge in risky business behavior. Intuition, confidence and experience play a major role when it comes to being risky with business investments.

5. **People may criticize you because you are so focused on making money or achieving the goals.** Don't worry about criticism. People will always have something to say. Tell them to mind their business because you are focused on grinding and growth in your industry.

6. **Pursuing success can cause you to sometimes feel out of touch with the real world.** When you are constantly working, you sometimes forget the real world. You can become so wrapped up in climbing the ladder of success that you only focus on accomplishing your checklist. You

don't know what's going on in the real world. You may not know what's going on in the world or your community because you have not been looking at the news or engaging socially due to your hectic work schedule.

Good Things About Success

1. **Achieving constant success can allow one to gain wealth.** It also helps build a legacy for your family and loved ones.

2. **The pursuit of success in your niche allows you to become a thought leader and influencer.** Your success will make room for you. You will become a sought-after speaker. The knowledge that you gain in your field may allow you to set trends within your industry.

3. **It's great to be able to become a mentor in your community and give back to others.** Becoming successful will allow you to inspire and motivate others to become successful. It will also allow you to share your knowledge and help someone else learn from your experiences.

4. **Being successful can help you become more fulfilled in life.** Once you have realized the success that you've always imagined, you will feel like you have made a genuine contribution to society by following your dreams.

5. **Success allows you to continuously improve yourself.** Becoming successful is tied to confidence and self-worth. To be successful, you must constantly reinvent yourself. If there is something that you want to improve, you will always have the means to do so. This will also allow you to keep achieving greatness.

6. **Success gives you the freedom to design or create the life you love.** You will be able to live a more confortable lifestyle. You will be able to travel and explore more of the world, without worrying about if you are jeopardizing your budget.

Push past your fears

Success is waiting on the other

side of your comfort zone!

CHAPTER 7

Deficiencies

A deficiency is a lack or a shortage. A lack of effort, motivation, focus, time, resources and confidence can delay us from meeting our highest potential in life. In order to solve these issues, we must first realize that these deficiencies exist. Then, we must look for ways to resolve these issues so that we may become whole. Let's take a closer look at these deficiencies.

1. A Lack of Effort

We all have times when we strive to accomplish goals, but we don't complete them. We talk about the things that we want to do with our family and close friends, but we don't act on them. It may not be intentional, but it is a self-defeating tactic to delay your purpose from being fulfilled. We must put our goals in writing. We have to plan and make our goals clear so that we can accomplish them. Sometimes, life is complicated. Life doesn't allow us to reach every goal that we want to achieve.

A lack of effort haunted me for years. I was never a stranger to great ideas and creativity. My mind was always turning. I always had a great idea, but I procrastinated and never brought my ideas to fruition. I always talked about the things that I wanted to accomplish, but I was afraid to make them happen. It was just that simple: failure to launch due to a lack of effort. I wrote out basic plans, but I was not motivated. So, I did not take immediate action to make my dream a reality.

2. Lack of Motivation

It's easy to write a list of goals. The hard part is getting motivated to accomplish the goals. Sometimes, we lack the drive to complete them. You may be around negative people, or you may be in a dry season. Sometimes, we have good ideas and it's simply not the right time to move on them. It's always good to have a notebook handy. Write the idea down and revisit it later.

Your circle of friends and associates play a major role in motivating you. Some people can drain you emotionally and mentally. Hang around positive people, with positive and encouraging attitudes. Some people constantly complain and always leave you feeling like a heavy burden is placed upon you just by their mere presence.

Other times, we may need an accountability partner. Collaborate with someone who you can trust, someone who will motivate you to tackle that goal. You can both encourage each other to make sure that you are meeting your deadlines. This works well for a person who may be busy and can easily get sidetracked.

3. Lack of Focus

Every now and then, you may have too much going on. Your mind is cluttered. When you have a specific goal that you want to accomplish, after you write out your plan, create a strategy to tackle it. You must set a deadline and do something every day until that goal is accomplished. Many have faced multiple failures, and they stay focused on the mistakes they have made in relationships, business and finances. We must learn to train our minds to stop replaying bad memories. We must imagine where we *want to be* instead of where we've been. Imagine success.

We must stop overthinking things. When we overthink, we rehash the past and we cannot move on to the positive things that we want to happen in our future. Refuse to rehash the past.

4. **A Lack of Resources**

Achieving your purpose may be expensive. It may take time for the complete goal to be accomplished. Sometimes, you may have to schedule projects in small increments until the bigger goal is accomplished. You may have to save money, borrow money or even apply for a loan or grant. You may even need to become creative and somehow make it all happen for free. After all, necessity is the mother of invention.

There are a few things to consider when dealing with a lack of resources. You may need to re-evaluate why you have a lack of resources. Can you use a less expensive substitution? Once you re-evaluate the situation, create a new budget based on the new findings. This readjustment should help to redirect needed funds and, hopefully, will make it easier to finance your project.

5. **A Lack of Confidence (Insecurity)**

Having a lack of confidence can rob a person of fulfilling their destiny. Insecurity leaves many people feeling like their gifts are not enough. Insecurity can cause a person to compare their life to someone else, leaving them wondering why it's taking so long to accomplish their dreams.

I think we all have been insecure at certain times in our lives. We've all felt unsure about certain things. That's when we need to take our burdens to God and pray that He will give us the courage and the strength to get to the finish line. I have felt insecure about pursuing certain goals, especially writing a book.

In 2008, while on vacation, I started writing a novel. I was laid out on the beach with a spiral notebook. I started writing a story about a young woman who was navigating through life to secure her place in the world. Like everyone else in young adulthood, she had issues with her relationship, and she was pursuing success in her career. So, I thought I was off to a good start. I wrote about eight chapters, and then I got discouraged. I started questioning if my work was good enough. I pondered if it would be interesting enough. I started wondering if it would change anyone's life or if it would change their way of thinking. I kept replaying all the scenarios that would cause me to fail. I was trying to tell the main character's story, but I felt that her family's story became a bit of a distraction. I didn't know how to make my main character shine, yet still give her sisters the spotlight.

My goal was to start a series of books about the main character's family. I was going to start out with the main character's story first, then lead in to her family's story. I got too frustrated trying to accomplish this goal. I needed a mentor or someone to help me with this process. I did some preliminary research and found a few authors groups on Facebook. I was excited when I found out about a local gathering and I planned to attend. I got off work early and headed to the event.

When I got to the event, there was a lot of other events going on at the venue, as well. I inquired about the group that I was supposed to be meeting, and I was told that the event was cancelled. I was so frustrated. I went home, feeling even more hopeless about my book. I tried to reach out to the organizer on Facebook, but she never responded. I was disappointed.

So, that situation, plus my frustration with feeling insecure about how to continue with the development of my story, caused me to lack confidence. I felt hopeless and I didn't want to finish the book. When I tried to get help, it was not available. This insecurity caused me to delay the completion of my first novel. The funny thing is I got constant reminders to finish the book throughout the years, but I ignored them. The story takes place in Detroit in 2008, and I have a part in the book about the Oakland County Health Department. Throughout the years, every time I would drive past the Oakland County Health Department on Greenfield between 12 and 13 Mile in Southfield, it was a constant reminder for me to finish my book. From 2008 to 2017, for the most part, I ignored the inner push. I didn't want to deal with my feelings of insecurity and overthinking about the book.

    I have started working on the book again and hope to complete it soon. I broke through my lack of confidence by becoming educated about the process of character development. The character inventory helped me to fully develop my characters. Listening to other authors share their experiences with writing novels has given me a new perspective. I am now able to confidently finish my novel. It is my goal to complete the story and turn it into a series. I can't wait for you to read it! The book has some great universal themes and life lessons. I hope it inspires others and changes lives.

Stop focusing on what everyone else is doing!

Focus on where you want to be

in the next six months!

Success is waiting for you!

Queashar L. Halliburton

CHAPTER 8

Self-Sabotaging Behaviors that Delay Success

Self-sabotaging behaviors are dream killers. They inadvertently show up and control your life by building barriers to block you from your goals. These addictive behaviors encourage you to make excuses. If you don't acknowledge and change your behavior, these bad habits will cause you to stall. Some of these self-sabotaging behaviors include having a negative mindset, living for someone else's approval, procrastination, living in fear, supporting someone else before you support yourself, observing others and living in the past.

1. **A Negative Mindset (Doubt)**

During your quest for success, life will bring many obstacles to impede your progress. We must know how to acknowledge, identify and make a solid plan to address these dream killers. One of the most debilitating challenges that we may face in our journey, is overcoming a negative mindset. Our minds are all-encompassing. The way that we think determines how much success we will experience.

If you think that you will never accomplish your goals, then you are right. Your negative mindset will keep you from fulfilling your God-given destiny. You must retrain your mind to think positive thoughts. For every negative thought that enters your brain, you must immediately combat it with a positive thought. When negativity tries to invade your mind, you must immediately speak against it. You can recite Philippians 4:13:

I can do all things through Christ which strengthens me.

A self-defeating mindset can be your worst enemy. Your mindset controls your actions. How you feel will determine if you will bring positive or negative energy to the table. Positive energy usually encourages action. If you feel positive about something, it causes you to be proactive. For instance, you may have an idea about something that you want to accomplish. You may start with Google, then you may search YouTube and find a video regarding your idea. Your research may cause you to start writing out plans to accomplish the idea. Then, on the other hand, if you feel negatively about something, this will cause you to shut down any creativity regarding that idea.

Years ago, there was a lot of negative publicity about the city of Detroit nationwide. I immediately thought of creating a project to help redirect the negativity and refocus the attention on some of the great aspects of this great city. I started to research the idea and I came up with a great spin on the topic. Then suddenly, I thought about all the roadblocks that could stop me from completing the project. I stopped before I even got started. I started to think negatively, and I told myself that I couldn't do it. It's crazy because I love to do research. All I had to do was do it. But, of course, I came up with too many excuses as to why I couldn't do it. As I am writing this, I am reigniting my desire to finish this project and putting it on my to-do list.

The main takeaway regarding the negative mindset is to immediately say something or think of something positive when a negative thought comes to your mind. You have to retrain your brain to be positive.

2. Living for Someone Else's Approval

Stop worrying about what someone else will say or how they will feel when you decide to follow your destiny. Do what God intended for you to do and stop focusing on other people's opinion about your dream. It really doesn't matter what they think. They are not worried about your opinion when it comes to living their lives. So, don't let another person's opinion of you ruin your life or cause you not to fulfill your purpose. Sometimes, we may even do this subconsciously. We may not be aware what we are doing. We must honestly evaluate how we feel about certain things and move according to how we feel.

Stop letting family and friends tell you what you like and what you should do. We need to learn to think for ourselves and be confident that we are making the best decisions for our lives. So many times, we get caught up doing things a certain way because we let other people's opinions dominate our thinking. Learn to weigh your options independently. Trust your gut and move forward with the best decision. There was a time when I felt that I had to check with other people before I made a move. I had unconsciously created this habit. I came up with ideas and I'd ask someone what they thought about the idea. I would only move, or not move forward, based on others' opinions. It was a self-defeating process.

3. Supporting Someone Else's Vision before You Accomplish Your Own

Don't get me wrong. It's nothing wrong with helping a family member, friend or associate. But when helping them constantly detours you from accomplishing your goal, you need to re-evaluate how you are spending your time. Set aside time to complete your goals first. Then, if you have time to help your family or friends, let them know when you are available.

For so many years, I was guilty of this. I helped friends with projects and I had my own projects that I needed to finish. I put my projects on the back burner as I watched others flourish. Then, I wondered why I was never getting ahead.

4. **Fear of Success or Failure**

You may ask yourself, "How could someone be scared of success?" Sometimes we fail to start because we are scared that we may fail at a certain task. Being successful is hard work. Once you have accomplished some success, people will hold you to a higher standard. People will now look for you to be innovative and make some important moves that can influence change in your field or industry. It sometimes causes pressure to be an achiever and help change the mindsets of your peers or people in your industry.

5. **Procrastination**

To procrastinate means to delay action. I've battled with procrastination for decades. In fact, this is my biggest downfall. Procrastination is a dream killer. It will have you thinking that you have plenty of time to accomplish your goal, while you waste your life in professional mediocrity. Professional mediocrity means being productive just enough to get by in life. You are not a total slacker, but you do just enough so that you will be just under the radar. Procrastination is a time stealer and it will have you in a stalled position.

Procrastination was my specialty. I used to make up excuses and tell myself that maybe it was not my time. For instance, I would get a great idea for business and I would write it down. I would tell my inner circle about the idea and then, I wouldn't do anything with it. I was constantly overthinking. I would plan to deal with it later. However, later never came. I had so many missed opportunities.

6. **Living in the Past**

We all wish we could go back to the past and change a few things. When you are so caught up in the past, when you keep rehashing your mistakes and failures or past successes and triumphs, you are not living in the present! Make it a priority to live and dwell in the present. When your mind is set on things of the past, you can't focus on the future. You can't plan for success because you are so caught up in the days of your past. For years, I was stuck in the past. I kept beating myself up because of missed opportunities and mistakes that I made in my career or relationships. I played it too safe in my life. I thrived in my own comfort zone and refused to live in the unknown. However, no one knew what I was going through. I had to be in total control and know the result before I agreed to it. I was not willing to take a chance. I just wasn't brave enough to chance it. That's why I lived vicariously through others.

7. **Observing Others**

Stop worrying about the next person—whether it be your family, friends or associates. One of the unique things of this current generation has been the introduction of social media. With the infiltration of social media, people are clocking everyone else's every move. Nothing is too private to post about nowadays. We hear about everything from relationships and careers, to going to the corner store for a bag of chips. The constant posting of pictures and tagging of locations becomes obsessive and, sometimes, people get pulled into the drama. It can, at times, become hypnotizing. We can waste so much time looking at what someone else is doing that we miss living our own lives.

Most people don't post about their everyday struggles and the challenges they face. We see the glitz and glamour, and we forget that these people are human. We all face adversity. No one has a perfect life, whether we post it on social media or not. I can admit that I got caught up in the cycle of watching what people were doing on social media, and it was time consuming. I saw people making all these moves in the business world and I was blown away!

Some of my friends have motivated me to do more. They've caused me to stop procrastinating and make things happen for myself.

8. **Overthinking**

Overthinking is the sister to procrastination. Paralysis by over analysis is another way to look at it. It causes you to be in a position of immobility. It will cause you to rehash your options until it becomes an obsession and you are right where you started: at square one. Procrastination and overthinking were my defense mechanisms of choice. Overthinking caused me to procrastinate. It could have been an idea to write a book or completing another project. I kept talking about what I wanted to do, and that was it. I was *all talk*. Then, I would see or hear about some of my peers who were accomplishing their goals. Then, I'd get depressed because I felt like everyone was getting ahead, but me. I kept rehashing what I should have done. I just kept telling myself, "Shar, one day you are going to do this and that." But, I wouldn't *do* a thing.

Then, I started getting older. I still didn't do what God was telling me to do. I would sometimes start a project, then put it aside. I would find another project to work on. This was a self-defeating mechanism that kept me in an unproductive state.

Was I scared of success? Was I scared that people would hold me to a higher standard and I would be forced to keep achieving greater? I helped other people accomplish their goals, but I always put my goals on the back burner.

Every now and then, I got bursts of inspiration and started working on a project. For instance, in 2008, I started working on a project. But then, something else came up. I put that project on hold to pursue another one, without completing the task at hand. It was a circular disaster. I could not stay focused.

I was a chronic procrastinator. For years, I delayed going back to school to complete my master's degree. I applied twice and got accepted both times to University of Detroit Mercy. I even applied and was admitted to the education program at Marygrove College.

I had accomplished some success in the corporate world. I'd maintained multiple professional licenses, including real estate and insurance licensing. I was paying my bills and taking care of myself physically. It was just that I had personal goals that I wanted to accomplish in life, and I was putting those to the wayside due to fear and procrastination.

In 2015, I decided enough was enough. I finally enrolled in graduate school and I am now working on completing my Master's of Science in Administration with a specialization in Leadership, at Central Michigan University. I am now accomplishing my goals and it feels great! Once I complete my degree, I hope to be able to teach at the collegiate level.

Stop comparing your life to others!

Focus on your unique gifts and

plan your own journey to success!

Queashar L. Halliburton

CHAPTER 9

A Modern-Day Study on Success

I conducted a survey on modern-day views about success. The survey titled "The Success Factor," was created on September 24, 2017. The purpose of the survey was to get personal views on success and factors that prevented people from achieving success in life. I had 158 participants who answered six questions about their views on success. Multiple answers could be selected for certain questions. I used a free account on Survey Monkey to collect my data.

The following questions were proposed:

- What is your definition of success?
- Do you feel like you are successful?
- Do you feel anxious about your success?
- What factors affect your success?

- What is the one thing holding you back from success?
- How do you maintain success?

Survey Question #1:

Q1 What is your definition of success?

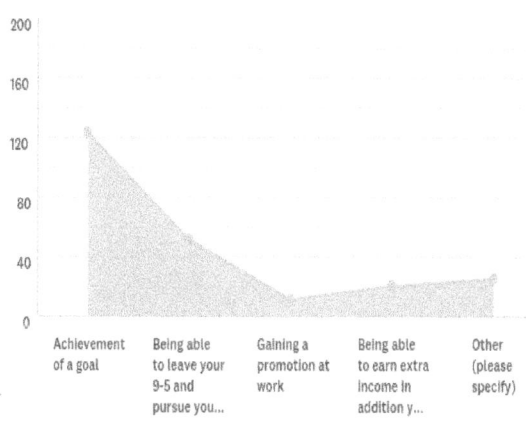

Results:

Multiple answers could be selected. Over 77 percent of respondents agree that success is the achievement of a goal. Approximately 32 percent of people surveyed believe that leaving your 9-to-5 job to pursue your dream full-time is proof of being successful.

- Approximately 15 percent of the people surveyed believed success was defined in other ways, such as:
  - "The ability to live comfortably and without debt, also in a secure space for growth."
  - "To have my own business"
  - "Being happy, doing what you love"
  - "Completing a goal"
  - "Creating a sustainable foundation of wealth"
  - "Being happy on your own terms"
  - "Also, a part of success is helping others to succeed"
  - "Discovering and walking into purpose"
  - "Seeing the results that I worked for"
  - "Achievement of a goal"
  - "Daily progress toward a goal"
  - "Living a happy life and living out God's purpose for your life"
  - "Achievement of a goal and being able to leave your 9-to-5 and pursue your dream full-time"
  - "Finding contentment"

- "Having a happy, loving family"
- "Being able to mentor someone to carry that goal forward"
- "Living, helping others, contentment"
- "Fulfilling your destiny"
- "Seeing your vision come to pass"
- "Self-actualization"
- "Success is being able to live happy, healthy and comfortably. All needs are met, with room to enjoy a satisfactory amount of wants."
- Approximately, 13 percent of people believe that success is being able to earn an additional income other than your primary job.
- Approximately, 7 percent of people believe that gaining a promotion at work proves that you are successful.

It was refreshing to read people's definition of success. This proves my point that success is relative to the individual. We all have things that are important to us. We have different desires and experiences that allow us to see things from a different perspective. For some, success has nothing to do with money. It's a feeling of security, safety and family. For others, success can be tied to achievements and have financial implications. Your definition of success will guide you to setting up an individual plan to accomplish your goals.

Survey Question #2:

Q2 Do you feel like you are successful?

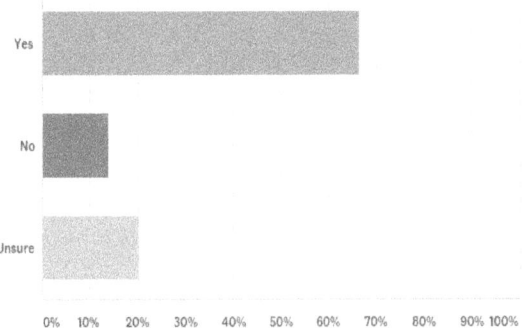

Results:

- Approximately, 66 percent said, "Yes, they feel successful."
- Approximately, 14 percent said, "No, they don't feel successful."

- Approximately, 20 percent said they felt unsure as to whether they are successful.

It's amazing that 66 percent of people feel that they are successful. That means that success is achievable. Since success is achievable, this should give us more confidence that we are equipped with all the things we need to achieve our goals. This gives me hope that most of the people surveyed are accomplishing their dreams.

Survey Question #3:

Q3 Do you feel anxious about your success?

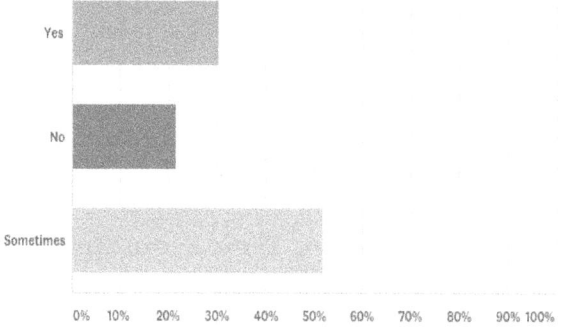

Results:

- Based on the findings, 30 percent of people said they feel anxious about their success.
- Approximately, 20 percent of the people surveyed said they are not anxious about their success.
- Approximately, 50 percent of people selected said they sometimes feel anxious about their success.

At least 80% percent of people surveyed feel anxious about achieving and maintaining success. Let's talk about anxiety and the implications of achieving success. Anxiety is defined as the feeling of nervousness or unease, typically about an imminent event or something with an uncertain outcome. So, achieving and maintaining success is something that can cause us to feel uneasy. We want to make sure that we are realizing our dreams in life, making an impact in this world, and that we can secure a decent standard of living for our family.

Anxiety causes mental distress or uneasiness because of fear of anger or perceived misfortune.

Survey Question #4:

Q4 What factors affect your success?

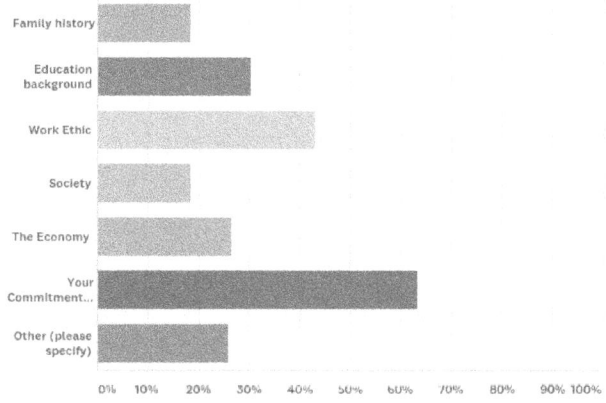

Results:

- Seven factors were included in the research question. Multiple factors could be selected.

- Approximately, 63 percent of people survey believed that one's commitment level affects success.

- Approximately, 43 percent said work ethic affects success.

- Approximately, 30 percent of people surveyed thought that your educational background affects your success level.
- Approximately, 27 percent said the economy affects your success.
- Approximately, 26 percent said that other factors affect your achievement of success, such as:
    - "Self-esteem"
    - "My 9-to-5"
    - "Spending habits"
    - "Work experience"
    - "Unknown factors"
    - "God's grace"
    - "Fear of success"
    - "Belief and confidence"
    - "Lack of resources"
    - "Availability"
    - "Writer's block"

- "Family history, educational background, work ethic, society, the economy, your commitment level"
- "My ability to believe in myself along with my capabilities. If I don't know something, I learn it or surround myself with others who do."
- "Health and self-sabotage"
- "My own insecurities"
- "Procrastination and energy level from a chronic condition"
- "Able to provide income for family"
- "Having the right steps to take action on"
- "Legacy"
- "Following the Holy Spirit's lead"
- "Temporary limited resources"
- "Health"
- "Energy"
- "Work/life balance"

Eighteen percent of people surveyed said that your family history also affects the level of success that you achieve.

- Approximately, 18 percent said society affects how successful you become.

Commitment level, work ethic and educational background, respectively, were the top elements that subjects felt affected their success the most. Over 60 percent of people feel that commitment is crucial to becoming successful. Consistency always wins!

Survey Question #5:

Q5 What is the one thing holding you back from becoming successful in life?

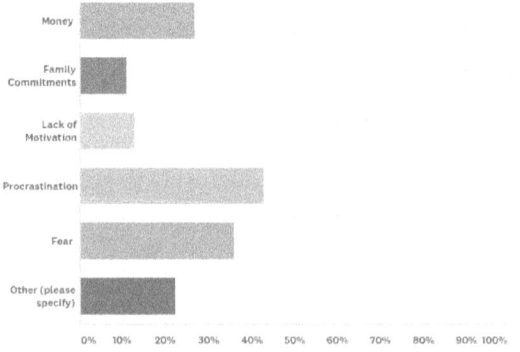

Results:

Multiple answers could be selected.

- Approximately, 36 percent said fear.
- Approximately, 27 percent said money.
- Approximately, 43 percent said procrastination.
- Approximately, 22 percent said other things, such as:
    - "Nothing" – (Four people wrote this answer)
    - "Time"
    - "Consistency"
    - "Health" (Two people wrote this answer)
    - "Ignorance. Few people even know how to set and achieve goals." "I'm finally overcoming fear, so few obstacles remain."
    - "Opportunity"
    - "Unknown"
    - "My 9-to-5"
    - "Mental roadblocks"
    - "Myself"
    - "All of the above"

- o "Autism"
- o "Lack of knowledge using the right tools"
- o "Just need to finish my action plan"
- o "Bad choices I've made in my past"
- o "I'm successful in many areas currently"
- o "Age and health"
- o "All of these hindrances can be overcome or ignored"

- Approximately, 13 percent lacked motivation.
- Approximately, 17 percent were affected by family obligations.

According to the survey, procrastination and fear are the top two things holding people back from achieving the success they desire in life. Others believe that bad choices that they made in their past, age and health issues affect how successful they can become in life. Procrastination and fear go hand in hand. Delaying your success due to these stumbling blocks has caused many to hold off on accomplishing and realizing their dreams. What is the real reason behind procrastination and fear? What are we afraid to do? Are we trying to avoid failure? Are we afraid of what people will think or say? We must overcome these self-defeating behaviors so that we can achieve and accomplish our goals and dreams.

Survey Question #6:

Q6 How do you maintain success?

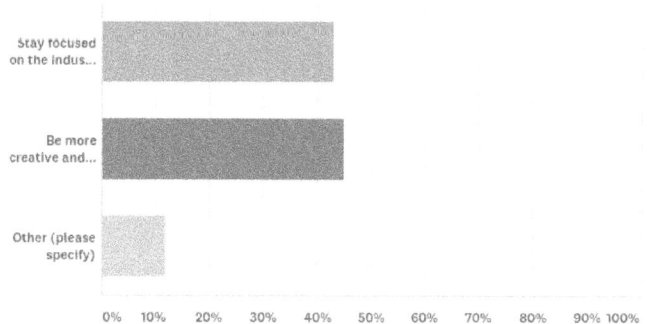

Results:

- Approximately, 43 percent of the people said they maintain success by staying focused on the industry and continually learning their trade.

- Approximately, 45 percent said they maintain success by being creative and innovative within their industry.
- Approximately, 1 percent said "Other," which yielded these results:
  - "Stay focused on the industry and keep learning your trade. Be creative and innovative within your industry."
  - "Come up with new ideas and focus on the now and what's next."
  - "It's a journey and you must reinvent yourself and try new things."
  - "Focus daily."
  - "Talk to people and share what you do. Give 80% and ask for them to buy a product at 20%."
  - "Find something that is important to me and focus."
  - "Learn to work with what I have. Start where I am. Work on one thing at a time daily. Pray and put God first."
  - "Find what works, implement it and grow a team to keep implementing it. Then, find the next thing that

works, implement it, rinse and repeat. I believe we all need to diversify ourselves to maintain success." "Nothing lasts forever, so we need to have our eggs in many different baskets."

- "Constantly follow God's lead and fail forward."
- "Continue to perfect your craft."
- "Always look ahead, never backward."
- "All of the above!"

Almost 50 percent of people surveyed believe that staying focused in their industry, and staying focused on trends in the industry, is key to maintaining success. Over one-third of the people surveyed believe that being creative within their industry helps people maintain success. Fourteen percent of the people surveyed had other ideas as it relates to maintaining success. In the next chapter, we will explore maintaining success and go a little deeper.

CHAPTER 10

Maintaining Success

Once you become successful, how do you maintain your success? Maybe developing a new concept or finding a quicker way to complete a long process, may help to maintain success in your industry. Perhaps taking a refresher class on a new phenomenon in your industry will get you up to speed on a new process.

Continue to read and study your craft. Consider subscribing to a new journal or business magazine that highlights trends in your industry. Listen to podcasts or consider creating one. Complete webinars and go to business development workshops or conferences.

Network with people in your niche and partner with people who have similar interests. Collaborate with business partners or associates who have similar interests. Partner with someone who has something that may complement your business. This way, you both mutually benefit from the new partnership efforts.

Become a mentor and help someone else become successful. With mentorship, you are reinforcing what you know, and you may even learn a new method or two in the process of teaching someone else your expertise.

Keep up with trends in your industry by keeping an active, open line of communication with other industry influencers.

Be forward thinking regarding your industry, trends and client needs. Talk to clients and ask them what they want and need. Then, develop new offerings based on the new interests of your market. Create an environment where business partners and clients feel free to express themselves and are open to growth and change.

CHAPTER 11

Ten Keys to Refocus, Reposition & Reclaim Your Purpose!

Since we have identified some of the stumbling blocks to success, we must identify ways to overcome the delays to success. Here are 10 actionable steps to revamp your life and skyrocket your success.

1.   Pray and ask God to identify your purpose in life. Take your cares and concerns to God. Ask for guidance and ask Him to place people in your life who will help you accomplish your dream or goal. Once you have identified your purpose, think of where you want to be in five years. Chart that out in your mind, then put it on paper. If you already know your purpose, refocus, reposition and reclaim your purpose in life. Forget about why you've stopped pursuing your dream. Take a deep breath. Get off the bench and get back in the game. Reignite the passion in your purpose.

2. **Don't share your dream with everyone.** Everyone will not be able to handle where God is taking you. Only share it with someone you can trust, someone you know has your best interest at heart. Some people will automatically become negative when they think you are trying to improve your life. They are comfortable with mediocrity and they want to stay comfortable. It's time for you to get out of your comfort zone. Throughout my career, I was blessed to have a boss who pushed me out of my comfort zone. By nature, I am a shy person at times. But my bosses all saw my potential and held me to a higher standard. Most gave me a leadership role and made me get out of my comfort zone. Those experiences made me grow and develop self-confidence. It helped propel me to the next level in my career. I am so grateful for the experiences.

3. **Get an accountability partner.** This should be someone who you trust. You can both freely set goals and

come up with timelines to accomplish those goals. Set up a time each week to check in with your accountability partner. It could be a phone call or a Skype session. You can also physically meet up once a week or twice a month. Set up a time that is realistic for you based on both of your schedules.

4. **Be creative with your finances.** You may need to research grants or loans, or even put money aside to save. Stop using lack of money as an excuse. Where there is a will, trust me, there is a way. You make it happen when you want to get that beautiful bag or shoes that you love. Make it happen when it comes to accomplishing your goals. You are well worth it, and you deserve the best that life has to offer, plus more.

5. **Invest in yourself.** If you don't think you are worth the investment, why would anyone else believe you are? If there is something that you can learn that will add more value to your expertise, go for it! You should be constantly improving and increasing your value. You are worth it! Be the best that you can be! Take classes, read books in your discipline,

listen to podcasts and attend workshops/conferences. Always hone your craft.

6. **Surround yourself and your network with positive friends and associates.** You may even have to make new friends with positive attitudes. Let go of people who drain your positive energy. Some people are always negative, and they change your mood and attitude as soon as they step within 5 feet of you. You can feel that negative energy or spirit when they pop in the room. Be a supportive and positive friend. Check in with your friends to make sure they are doing well. Stop waiting for people to call you. You call them. Make sure that they are doing well. See if there is something that you can do to encourage them or make their day extra special. Trust me when I tell you that the favor will be returned when you least expect it from someone who you had no idea cared about you and your well-being.

7. **Take care of yourself mentally, physically and spiritually.**

Remove distractions. Remove anything that will stop you from following through with your goals and dreams. Toxic people need to go, as well. Do what you need to do to get mentally free of anything and everything that is holding you in a state of doing nothing.

Carve out time each day for self-care. Even if it's only 30 minutes, carve that time out. Great self-care is necessary. Take some quiet time and reflect. Your mental health and peace of mind is at stake. You cannot be the best you that you can be if you have not addressed mental health issues.

Take care of yourself mentally. Everyone needs to have someone to talk to, especially when you are feeling depressed. Don't be too proud to speak to a professional. There is a stigma in the black community when it comes to seeking help for mental health. Don't be afraid to go see a mental health professional. Most health insurance plans include outpatient mental health visits with low copays.

Don't be afraid to say, "No" when you need to. You are in control of your time clock outside of your work day. The ability to be in control of your time will free up your schedule to work on the things that you need to work on. This is one of the things that I constantly deal with. I am always doing toomuch.com. I love volunteering and helping others. But sometimes, I overdo it. You must always take into consideration your time and your mental health. We must home in on the thing that we want to accomplish and go for it full speed ahead. You must also be consistent and disciplined. Set aside time to do the things that you enjoy. Stop waiting for a holiday or your birthday to celebrate your accomplishments. Live your best life every day, without apologies and explanations. You are the architect of your life. You design the life that you love. Love yourself unconditionally, without regret. Do things that help build your confidence. Don't wait for others to do things to make you feel good.

Take time to stretch and exercise daily. Power walking in the morning really helps. If you are not a runner, a brisk power walk will give you a great start in the morning. It does wonders for me. It gives me time to think and improves my clarity when making important decisions. Breathing in the clear, fresh air helps to rejuvenate your body from the previous night's sleep. You owe it to yourself to take care of your temple.

Take time to prepare healthy meals. Your body is your temple, so treat it accordingly. Act like you love your body and your body will appreciate you for the tender loving care.

If you feel like you are gaining weight, do things to lose weight. Start making healthier food choices. Eat to live. Don't live to eat. If you can't run, start power walking or ride an exercise bike. Do what you can to change your situation. Make better choices for your health. You have total control over your circumstances.

Take pride in your appearance. Always look your best. Make sure that you have a well-groomed appearance. You never know whom you may run into while you are making your rounds. It's so easy to find a decent wardrobe at reasonable cost. Find your style and enhance it with a little makeup and a few jeweled statement pieces.

8. **Your journey is as unique as you are. Stop comparing your journey and secretly competing with others**. You are unique, and your journey will be completely different from your bestie's journey. Stop worrying about how your neighbor's sister's cousin made it big. Focus on the steps that you need to take to make it big. Stop stalking people's social media accounts and being obsessed with their every move. Make your own moves. Life is not great for everyone, every day. Most people only show the good times on social media. Everyone has silent struggles and obstacles. You would be surprised what people go through daily behind closed doors. The same person you are obsessively watching is the same person who is having an anxiety attack in the privacy of their own home. You never know what people are going through mentally, physically, financially and spiritually. People are fighting battles every day and we don't even know about it. People are fighting

depression and dealing with some major issues that we may never even know about unless they share openly. People are great at hiding their struggles. They choose to deal and heal in silence. Just focus on you. Work on the things that you need to accomplish so that you can one day reach out to someone who may need your help.

9. Stay relevant in your industry or specialty. Visualize, strategize, document and then execute your dream. Accomplish your goals, keep learning and honing your gifts. Create a daily routine that works well for you. Document the process that works. Follow the same steps that you created to complete a task until you are finished. Tweak the plan if you need to, repeat and reevaluate your progress.

Revise your plan, when necessary. Come up with a plan to accomplish the goal. Set realistic goals. It may take a few years to accomplish the big picture, so set up mini goals with deadlines. Check the completed goals off as you accomplish them.

10. Celebrate every victory. You will accomplish your goals and live life abundantly. Celebrate each step of the way. Once you find out what your purpose is, celebrate. Plan, and then celebrate. Start checking off and completing your tasks, then celebrate. Celebrate, celebrate, then rinse and repeat by celebrating. You deserve it. You are God's greatest creation and you are destined for greatness. Acknowledge your weaknesses. Accentuate your strengths. Be confident and skyrocket your success.

I wrote *Skyrocket Your Success* to help professional women acknowledge and identify self-sabotaging behaviors that are standing in the way of success. I want you to avoid years of feeling empty. Do what you need to do today to thrive and soar. For years, I worried about when my time was coming. I pondered about why I was not seeing the success that I dreamed about.

I didn't understand what was holding me back. I blamed situations and circumstances, and I didn't take ownership in my part of my delay. I never realized that I was holding myself back from greatness. I always played it safe and I wasn't willing to take any risks. I held myself back. I delayed my own success. I had all the potential, but I didn't pursue my entrepreneurial goals. I let procrastination, fear and self-doubt stop me from accomplishing my goals.

I was literally standing on the sidelines of life and watching others glow up. I was angry with myself because I was not where I wanted to be in life. I was depressed and oppressed. I would cry myself to sleep at night and I had insomnia. I could not tap into my inner power to achieve my goals. I felt zombie-like, just living day to day in a circle of unhappiness. Something had to change, and I was suffering in silence. I knew that a change had to start with me. I got tired of simply existing and I had to do something to change my life.

Learn to love yourself unapologetically. You are a unique gift, unlike any other. Embrace what makes you different. If there is something that you can improve, do it. Do whatever is within reason that helps build your self-confidence.

Take your God-given gifts and abilities and monetize on them. If there is something that you have a desire to do in business, go after it aggressively. The first thing you need to do is research. Then, determine where you need help. Don't feel that you must do everything alone. Get a mentor or coach to help you along the way. You will have to invest in yourself and it will be well worth it.

Pursue your dream vigorously. Don't let the naysayers control your moves. If you've prayed about it, and you know that this is what you want to do, then silence the negativity and move forward without regret.

If I had just been confident enough when I was younger, I feel that I would have went further sooner in life. I was always worried about what others thought about me and what I was doing. I needed to get outside of my comfort zone.

I had to acknowledge that I was the main reason that I was not following my dreams. I had to stop making excuses and just do what I needed to do. I had to forget about what others were thinking and pursue my dream.

The first thing that I had to do was pray and ask God to help me. I had to acknowledge my deficiencies and my strengths. I knew that I was feeling inadequate because there was so much more to my life. Since I was a child, I knew that I would make a difference in this world. I had gifts inside of me, yet I was not using them efficiently and effectively. I had a gift of creativity. I literally had to push myself into purpose.

For years, I felt a push into greatness, but I just ignored it. It disturbed me. I had many sleepless nights. God was prompting me to hone into the gifts that He had placed inside of me. It was time to let them out. I had to stop being scared to do the things that I was purposed to do. It all started with writing this book. I've had so much bottled up for years and I felt like I was going to burst.

I had to know that my story was good enough to share, and I just had to do it. I don't have a tragic story. I just know that I was not living my best life. I was letting mental and emotional roadblocks stop me from stepping out of my comfort zone and pursue my purpose fully. I was not happy because it made me depressed when I thought about the possibility that I could leave this life and not achieve my purpose. I wanted to share my story with other women and encourage them to not let fear, procrastination and doubt stop them. I finally feel free and hope this book has encouraged at least one woman to stop living in fear. Pursue greatness today.

I hope this book has helped you to think about your life. Level up and pursue your God-given gifts that you have been delaying in your life. You are so much more than your 9-to-5 job. There are specific things that you were born to accomplish in this life. Pursue your dreams and live life abundantly!

THE NEXT STEPS

I hope this book has motivated, inspired and empowered you to move forward and continue to attain greatness. If you would like the accompanying workbook to *Skyrocket Your Success*, or if you have further inquiries, please contact Queashar Halliburton at hello@sharhalliburton.com or visit www.sharhalliburton.com.

Stay connected with Queashar and Queashar Detroit Publishing on social media at:

Facebook: www.facebook.com/qdpublishing

LinkedIn: www.linkedin.com/in/queasharhalliburton

Twitter: www.twitter.com/qdpublishing

Instagram: www.instagram.com/qdpublishing

REFERENCES

Chapter 4- Warren Buffet- Business Insider, Áine Cain, September 1, 2017, https://www.businessinsider.com/warren-buffett-daily-routine-2017-8

Chapter 4-Jack Dorsey- Business Insider, Anisa Purbasari, July 31, 2016,3:00 AM, https://www.businessinsider.com.au/jack-dorsey-morning-routine-experiment-surprising-discovery-2016-7

Chapter 4- Oprah Winfrey- Business Insider- Valerie Rind, April 1. 2017, 11:01 AM https://amp.businessinsider.com/the-first-thing-15-highly-successful-people-do-each-morning-2017-3

Chapter 4- Michelle Obama- Business Insider, Gus Lubin and Rachel Gillett, September 12, 2016, 9:34 AM https://www.businessinsider.com/successful-people-whorag-wake-up-really-early-2016-4

ABOUT THE AUTHOR

While many neglect to follow their dreams due to setbacks like procrastination, fear and a lack of resources, she uses those very things as stepping stones to her success. For Queashar L. Halliburton, CEO and founder of Queashar Detroit Publishing, LLC, her greatest success to date has come from living outside the box and operating in her God-given gifts and purpose—and she encourages others to do the same. In addition to producing her fair share of personal literary works, she works diligently to provide tools, resources and motivation for new authors nationwide—positioning them to tell their stories in excellence and excel in the marketplace.

After 22 years in Corporate America—working in every field from education, insurance and real estate, to construction, sales and public relations—Queashar knew it was time for a shift. Blazing the trail for many, she founded Queashar Detroit Publishing in 2017, where she doesn't just seek to build a database of clientele. Educating them about the publishing process, marketing, building an author platform and more, she takes the time to go above and beyond the services other small publishers offer. Whereas many publishers focus on the end product, Queashar is committed to client education and great customer service—what many would consider to be a lost art. And her feature in a segment called "Sidewalk Talk" on *The Splash*, Greater West Bloomfield's News Magazine show, was just the beginning of many open doors.

Her love for authorpreneurs and entrepreneurs alike led the way for her to be a featured guest on numerous podcasts, including The Authors Podcast with Coach Robyn Robbins, the She Leads Podcast with Nicole Walker, and the Godlywood Girl TV YouTube Show with Stephanie Rodnez, CEO of Godlywood Girl. In addition to serving as a faithful member of the Nonfiction Authors Association, Queashar is also a member of the Advance Magazine Contributor Network, where her content will be featured throughout 2019 and beyond.

www.ingramcontent.com/pod-product-compliance
Lightning Source LLC
Chambersburg PA
CBHW020912090426
42736CB00008B/603